My Shell

For Simon

For a free color catalog describing Gareth Stevens' list of high-quality books, call 1-800-542-2595 (USA) or 1-800-461-9120 (Canada). Gareth Stevens' Fax: (414) 225-0377.

Library of Congress Cataloging-in-Publication Data

Patchett, Lynne.
   My Shell / by Lynne Patchett; photographs by Fiona Pragoff.
      p.   cm. — (First step science)
   Includes bibliographical references (p. 31) and index.
   ISBN 0-8368-1188-7
   1. Shells—Juvenile literature. [1. Shells.] I. Pragoff, Fiona. II. Title. III. Series.
   QL405.2.P38   1995
   574.4'7—dc20   94-34040

This edition first published in 1995 by
Gareth Stevens Publishing
1555 North RiverCenter Drive, Suite 201
Milwaukee, Wisconsin 53212, USA

This edition © 1995 by Gareth Stevens, Inc. Original edition published in 1991 by A & C Black (Publishers) Ltd., 35 Bedford Row, London WC1R 4JH. © 1991 A & C Black (Publishers) Ltd. Photographs © 1991 Fiona Pragoff, except p. 22 Robert Pickett. Additional end matter © 1995 by Gareth Stevens, Inc.

Series editor: Patricia Lantier-Samp a
Editorial assistants: Mary Dykstra, Diane Laska
Illustrations: Mandy Doyle
Science consultant: Dr. Bryson Gore

Printed in the United States of America
1 2 3 4 5 6 7 8 9 99 98 97 96 95

My Shell

by Lynne Patchett
photographs by Fiona Pragoff

Gareth Stevens Publishing
MILWAUKEE

Look at all the colors and patterns on these shells.

How many shapes and sizes can you see?

My shell is big and has stripes.

I can hear
the sea!

6

My shell is bumpy on the outside . . .

and smooth on the inside.

We're tracing around our shells.

How many patterns can you see?

My shell winds
in a coil shape.

If I blow into my shell,
I can make music.

11

My shell floats this side up.
Will it float if I turn it over?

Most of these shells sink in water.

This shell has
a fan shape.

It has two pieces.
They fit together
like this.

15

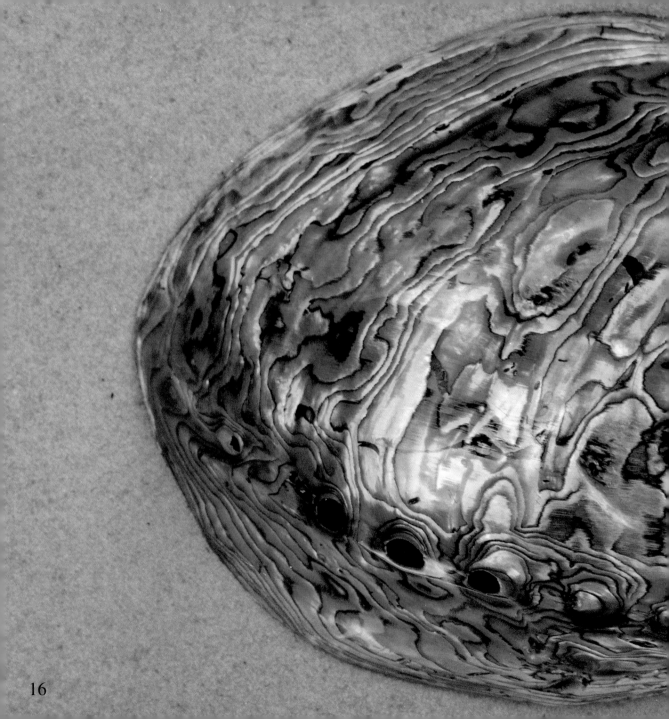

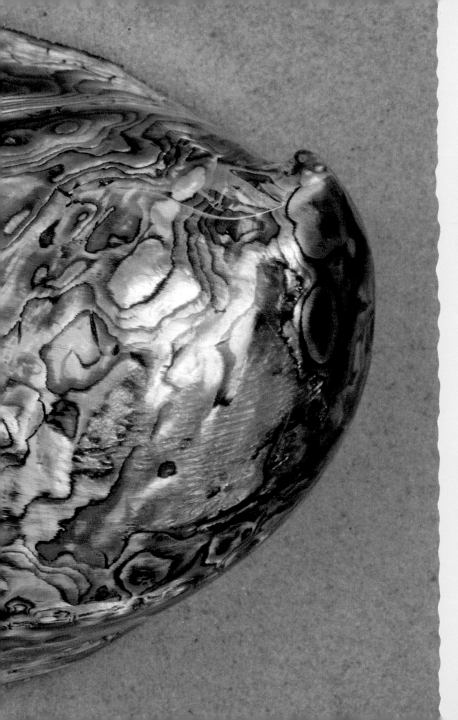

The outside of
this shell is like
a rainbow.

How many colors
can you see?

We're making a shell box.

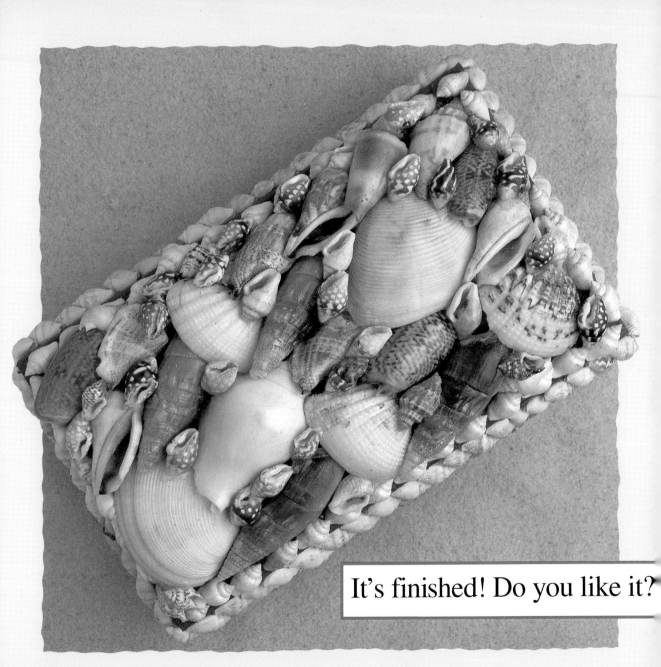

It's finished! Do you like it?

Some types of shells grow on trees.
They have prickly cases.

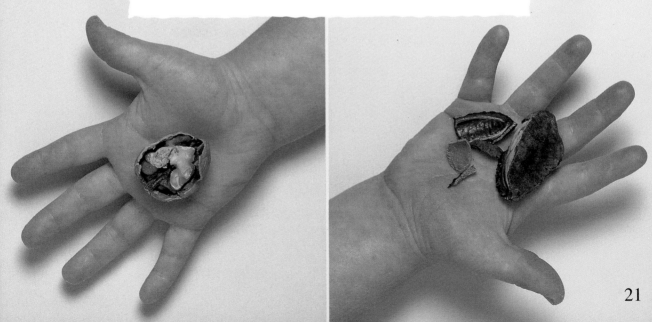

These shells came from trees, too.
Look what we found inside.

21

Chicks hatch out of eggs with shells.

This snail has a shell on its back.

We're making a shell sand castle.

Can you find my shell?

FOR MORE INFORMATION

Notes for Parents and Teachers

As you share this book with young readers, these notes may help you explain the scientific concepts behind the different activities.

pages 4, 5, 8, 9, 10, 14-17, 24, 25
Colors and shapes

Shells come in many colors and shapes that work to protect them by blending in with their natural environment.

pages 4, 5, 9, 10, 14, 15, 18-25
Kinds of shells

Shells are hard outer casings that protect animals such as mollusks, crabs, turtles, and tortoises, as well as baby birds and certain plant fruits. Some mollusk shells (univalves) are one piece coiled in a spiral shape. Others (bivalves) are divided into two parts that may be equal (mussels) or unequal (scallops) in size.

pages 7, 14, 16-17
Textures of shells

The outside texture of a mollusk shell may help make the shell strong to protect the animal. The shell's inside is usually smooth and pearly. A mollusk shell is part of the body of the animal. It is formed by a thin layer called the mantle, which is between the soft body of the animal and the hard shell. The shell is made of calcium carbonate (limestone).

page 10
Growth and coiling

Mollusk shells grow bigger as the animal inside them grows. Some shells have growth rings like those in tree trunks. Coiled univalves add spirals as they grow. Most spiral shells coil to the right. Rings or spirals on a shell can be counted to give some idea of its age.

pages 6, 11 Sound and music

When we hold a shell to one ear, the swishing sound we hear is the air vibrating and bouncing around inside an enclosed space. The vibrations inside the shell are triggered by some of the vibrations in the air around us. This is called resonance. Blowing into a shell also makes the air vibrate to produce a sound. Musical instruments with pipes, such as trumpets, work in a similar way.

pages 12, 13
Floating and sinking

A floating object displaces a volume of water weighing the same as its own weight.

pages 20, 21
Nuts from trees

The hard shells around tree nuts help protect the seed or seeds inside. There is also a store of food inside the nut, which helps the tree start growing.

page 22 Birds' eggs

Birds lay eggs that have a hard shell. Many birds build nests to protect their eggs. Birds that don't build nests often lay eggs that have camouflage markings.

page 23 Snail shells

Snails move on a flat, muscular foot. On the back of the foot is a structure called the operculum, which is used like a trapdoor to close the shell entrance when the snail goes inside.

Things to Do

1. Collecting shells

Stay on the lookout for shells in gardens, on outside walls, or on beaches at low tide. Collect only empty shells, and put back any living shells you find. Make a note of where and when you found the shells. To clean the shells, soak them in hot water for a while, and then rinse them under cold running water. See if you can find out the names of your shells and then label them. Sort your collection into groups of the same type or size. Keep the shells safe by storing them in boxes, plastic containers, or tins with a layer of cotton cloth inside.

2. Fossil hunting

You can sometimes find very old shells buried in rock. Some of the animals that once lived in the shells may have been alive during the days of the dinosaurs. These old shells are called fossils.
Try saying:

"She sells seashells on the
    seashore.
The shells she sells are seashells
    I'm sure."

This tongue twister is about a young woman named Mary Anning, a famous fossil hunter.

3. Shell design

Shells and shell patterns are often used in advertising and product design. Look for shell designs in products displayed in your local supermarket or in magazine advertising. Create and draw a new product that uses the shape of a seashell.

Fun Facts about Shells

1. A seashell, or mollusk shell, is formed by the mantle of the animal living inside. A mantle is a thick fold of skin that surrounds the animal's body. As the animal grows, the mantle secretes the materials that make up the shell, and the shell expands outward.

2. In water, the shells of clams, oysters, and other bivalves open a little to let in water. The water carries food and minerals to the animals inside the shells.

3. Long ago, the people of Greece used certain shells to make a purple dye. This dye was used to make beautiful fabric for clothing.

4. Some shells carry other, smaller shells on top of themselves as protection. As you might guess, the larger shells are called carrier shells.

5. In some parts of the world, such as Indonesia, large shells are sometimes used as bathtubs.

6. Some clam shells are very large, and others are very small. A giant clam shell can be over 4 feet (1.2 meters) across, but a nut clam shell is only about as wide as your finger.

7. In some parts of Africa, cowrie shells are strung together to make rattles. Cowrie shells are also used as money in some parts of the world.

8. Large shells are sometimes used as musical instruments.

Glossary

case — a container or box.

chick — a baby bird.

coil — a single or series of spiral or ring-shaped patterns.

fan — a semicircular object used to stir up air, usually for the purpose of cooling things off.

float — to stay on the surface of a liquid, such as water.

hatch — to be born from an egg.

patterns — designs or prints.

prickly — pointed and stinging, like thorns on a bush.

sea — a body of saltwater; ocean.

shell — a hard, protective covering; many animals and seeds have shells.

sink — to fall beneath the surface of a liquid instead of floating on top.

snail — a type of slow-moving animal that belongs to a group called mollusks. Snails have spiral shells.

stripes — long, thin bands of alternating or different colors that may be placed next to each other to form a design or pattern.

trace — to draw the outline of an object.

wind — to wrap, bend, or twist thread, rope, or some other material around an object or some other central point.

Places to Visit

Everything we do involves some basic scientific principles. Listed below are a few museums that offer a variety of scientific information and experiences. You may also be able to locate other museums in your area. Just remember: you don't always have to visit a museum to experience the wonders of science. Science is everywhere!

American Museum of Natural
   History
Central Park West at 79th Street
New York, NY 10024

Shell Museum and Educational
   Foundation, Inc.
P.O. Box 1580
Sanibel, FL 33957

Royal Ontario Museum
100 Queen's Park
Toronto, Ontario
M5S 2C6

Royal British Columbia Museum
675 Belleville Street
Victoria, British Columbia
V8V 1X4

More Books to Read

A House for Hermit Crab
   Eric Carle
   (Picture Book Studio)

Seashells
   R. Tucker Abbot
   (Thunder Bay Press)

Seashore
David Burnie
(Dorling Kindersley)

Snails
Sylvia Johnson
(Lerner)

Shells
Jennifer Coldrey
(Dorling Kindersley)

What Lives in a Shell?
Kathleen Weidner Zoehfeld
(HarperCollins)

Videotapes

Living Seas
(Coronet)

What's Under the Ocean?
(Now I Know . . . About the
World of Science Video)

Index